John McCain

John McCain

by Gail B. Stewart

LUCENT BOOKS
A part of Gale, Cengage Learning

GALE
CENGAGE Learning

Detroit • New York • San Francisco • New Haven, Conn • Waterville, Maine • London

LIBRARY OF CONGRESS CATALOGING-IN-PUBLICATION DATA

Stewart, Gail B. (Gail Barbara), 1949-
  John McCain / by Gail B. Stewart.
    p. cm. — (People in the news)
  Includes bibliographical references and index.
  ISBN 978-1-4205-0055-4 (hardcover)
1. McCain, John, 1936—Juvenile literature. 2. Legislators—United States—Biography—
Juvenile literature. 3. United States. Congress. Senate—Biography—Juvenile literature.
4. Prisoners of war—Vietnam—Biography—Juvenile literature. 5. Prisoners of war—
United States—Biography—Juvenile literature. 6. United States Naval Academy—
Biography—Juvenile literature. 7. Presidential candidates—United States—Biography—
Juvenile literature. I. Title.
  E840.8.M26S74 2008
  328.73092—dc22
  [B]
                                                                            2008011403

Lucent Books
27500 Drake Rd
Farmington Hills MI 48331

ISBN-13: 978-1-4205-0055-4
ISBN-10: 1-4205-0055-4

Printed in the United States of America
4 5 6 7 12 11 10 09

Contents

Fame and celebrity are alluring. People are drawn to those who walk in fame's spotlight, whether they are known for great accomplishments or for notorious deeds. The lives of the famous pique public interest and attract attention, perhaps because their experiences seem in some ways so different from, yet in other ways so similar to, our own.

Newspapers, magazines, and television regularly capitalize on this fascination with celebrity by running profiles of famous people. For example, television programs such as *Entertainment Tonight* devote all their programming to stories about entertainment and entertainers. Magazines such as *People* fill their pages with stories of the private lives of famous people. Even newspapers, newsmagazines, and television news frequently delve into the lives of well-known personalities. Despite the number of articles and programs, few provide more than a superficial glimpse at their subjects.

Lucent's People in the News series offers young readers a deeper look into the lives of today's newsmakers, the influences that have shaped them, and the impact they have had in their fields of endeavor and on other people's lives. The subjects of the series hail from many disciplines and walks of life. They include authors, musicians, athletes, political leaders, entertainers, entrepreneurs, and others who have made a mark on modern life and who, in many cases, will continue to do so for years to come.

These biographies are more than factual chronicles. Each book emphasizes the contributions, accomplishments, or deeds that have brought fame or notoriety to the individual and shows how that person has influenced modern life. Authors portray their subjects in a realistic, unsentimental light. For example, Bill Gates —the cofounder and chief executive officer of the software giant Microsoft—has been instrumental in making personal computers the most vital tool of the modern age. Few dispute his business savvy, his perseverance, or his technical expertise, yet critics say he is ruthless in his dealings with competitors and driven more by his desire to maintain Microsoft's dominance in the computer industry than by an interest in furthering technology.

In these books, young readers will encounter inspiring stories about real people who achieved success despite enormous obstacles. Oprah Winfrey—the most powerful, most watched, and wealthiest woman on television today—spent the first six years of her life in the care of her grandparents while her unwed mother sought work and a better life elsewhere. Her adolescence was colored by promiscuity, pregnancy at age fourteen, rape, and sexual abuse.

Each author documents and supports his or her work with an array of primary and secondary source quotations taken from diaries, letters, speeches, and interviews. All quotes are footnoted to show readers exactly how and where biographers derive their information and provide guidance for further research. The quotations enliven the text by giving readers eyewitness views of the life and accomplishments of each person covered in the People in the News series.

In addition, each book in the series includes photographs, annotated bibliographies, timelines, and comprehensive indexes. For both the casual reader and the student researcher, the People in the News series offers insight into the lives of today's newsmakers—people who shape the way we live, work, and play in the modern age.

A Proud History

Many who know John McCain say it is impossible to get a full sense of who he is without understanding his family history. It makes it clear why he has chosen the path he is on—from serving the U.S. military in Vietnam to serving as a U.S. senator to seeking the Republican Party's nomination for president of the United States in 2000 and again in 2008. "For John," says McCain supporter Robert Childs, "life is about honor and about serving the country. That's who he is today, that's who he was in Vietnam and that's who he has been ever since. It's all about honor and service."[1]

A Five-Year-Old's Memory

McCain himself says that one of his first memories, at age five, gave him an idea of what such service meant. It was a Sunday morning, December 7, 1941, when the McCain family lived in New London, Connecticut. His father, a navy submariner, was stationed there, for although World War II was raging in Europe, the United States was not a part of it.

However, things changed that morning, says McCain. A black car driven by a naval officer pulled up in front of their house. The officer yelled to McCain's father that the Japanese had just sunk the American fleet at Pearl Harbor, Hawaii. The United States was suddenly at war. "My father left for the base immediately," recalls McCain. "I saw very little of him for the next four years."[2]

Of course, for millions of Americans, service in 1941 meant enlisting in the armed forces. It meant being wrenched away from home and family as they fought enemies in Asia and Europe. And while that was hard for young John McCain to understand at age five, he would later learn that McCains had been doing that since before the American Revolution.

A Long History of Military Service

In fact, as John grew up, he learned that the McCain family had a history of military service that went back to colonial times. Two McCain ancestors, brothers John and Thomas Young, both served in the Augusta County, Virginia, militia, where they fought a brief skirmish with Indian forces at the Battle of Back Creek in 1764. After Thomas was killed and scalped, John was able to survive, and he spent the next three days tracking those responsible for his brother's death. When he caught up with them, he resumed the battle and was able to reclaim the scalp and buried it with his brother's body.

"No one in my family is certain if we are descended from an unbroken line of military officers," writes McCain in his

Slew McCain

The first John Sidney McCain became a four-star admiral in the U.S. Navy. He was known as Slew to his fellow officers (though his grandson never knew why). The men serving under him referred to him by a different name: Popeye. The reference was to an old cartoon character, because of a misshapen green sailor cap McCain wore during combat missions. He was something of a character, too, with poorly fitting false teeth that gave his speech a rhythmic clicking and whistling sound. Such idiosyncrasies aside, McCain was a brilliant strategist and naval hero, serving in both World War I and World War II.

John McCain sits on the lap of his grandfather, Admiral
John S. McCain Sr., in a family portrait, with his sister
Alexandra, father John S. McCain Jr., and mother Roberta.

memoir *Faith of My Fathers*. "But you can trace that heritage through many generations of our *family*, finding our ancestors in every American War."[3]

The most famous McCains of all were his grandfather and father, who both achieved the rank of four-star admirals in the navy. Their heroic accomplishments—spanning two world wars—were legends in the McCain family. Raised with such tradition, it is little wonder that as a boy, McCain says his imagination, "would conjure up some future day of glory when I would add my own paragraph to the family's legend."[4]

A Different Idea of Service

And while McCain did serve in the navy, he has also redefined his family's idea of service. By running for political office—first as a congressman, then senator, and then two bids for president of the United States, McCain has expanded his view of what service to his country means. He says he can make a difference and serve the United States in a way different than anyone in his family has done before.

"I know how the world works," he said as he announced his candidacy for president in 2007. "I know the good and the evil in it. I know how to work with leaders who share our dreams of a freer, safer, and more prosperous world, and how to stand up to those who don't."[5]

He has a long list of opponents, and McCain is certainly not the most heavily funded of the Republican candidates. But if that concerns him, he does not show it. He remains confident that he is the best person for the job. As the 2008 presidential election nears, he is eager, at age seventy-one, to do what he dreamed of as a boy—to add his own paragraph to the McCain family legend.

Chapter 1

Young Johnny McCain

John Sidney McCain III was born on August 29, 1936, at a Panama naval air base called Coco Solo. His father, John Jr. (known as Jack), was a navy officer stationed at a submarine facility nearby. His grandfather, the senior John Sidney McCain, was commander of the naval base at the time. For a short time, the three generations of McCains were together.

A Wandering Life

A few months later, his father was transferred again. As he grew, young John McCain found that it was part of the life of a navy family—transfers were common. Families tried as hard as they could to stay together, but being uprooted on a regular basis was especially difficult for the children.

"The repeated farewells to friends rank among the saddest regrets of a childhood constantly being disrupted by my father's career," McCain later wrote. "I would arrive at a new school, go to considerable lengths to make new friends, and shortly thereafter, be transplanted to a new town to begin the process all over again."[6]

Not only were friends difficult to keep, but even when the family resided together at the base, his father was gone most of the time. Long weeks at sea, even during peacetime, were just part of the job of a navy submariner. McCain says that as a little boy, at the same time he idolized his father, he grew resentful of

A young John McCain (center) with his grandfather, Admiral John S. McCain Sr. (left), father Commander (later admiral) John S. McCain Jr., and younger brother Joe in a family photo from the 1940s.

his long absences, interpreting them as a sign that he loved his career more than he loved his children. "That was unfair of me," he says now, "and I regret having felt that way."[7]

"Get the Water!"

Another regret is his quick temper—something that has been part of his personality for his entire life. Johnny (as he was known to his family) began to show that temper as a little boy—in ways that both frightened and perplexed his parents. The slightest thing could set him off. He would rant and scream, and then suddenly fall to the floor—totally unconscious.

Concerned that this might be some medical problem, his parents took him to a doctor at the base. The doctor told them it was nothing medical. Johnny was not sick—his lapses into unconsciousness were caused by his being angry, and holding his breath until he passed out. The doctor advised them to fill a bathtub with cold water, and whenever Johnny began working himself into a rage and appeared to be holding his breath, to simply drop him into it, fully clothed.

McCain's memories of the doctor's therapy are pretty vivid. Whenever he began to show signs of a tantrum, he says, "my mother shouted to my father, 'Get the water!' Moments later I would find myself thrashing, wide-eyed and gasping for breath, in a tub of icy-cold water."[8]

Mother in Charge

With his father gone so much, it was McCain's mother who raised the children—Johnny, his sister Sandy, and his brother Joe. Like many navy wives of that time, she was more than capable of handling things on her own. From nursing the children through sore throats and chicken pox, to buying

The McCain children were raised almost exclusively by their mother, as their father was gone for long periods while serving in the U.S. Navy. Pictured here is 2-year-old John McCain and his sister Sandy in 1938.

His Mother's Son

In his family memoir, *Faith of My Fathers*, John McCain says that though he followed in his father's footsteps as far as his career, he was in temperament much more like his mother—something that makes him very proud.

> I became my mother's son. What I lacked of her charm and grace I made up for by emulating and exaggerating other of her characteristics. She was loquacious, and I was boisterous. Her exuberance became rowdiness in me. She taught me to find so much pleasure in life that misfortune could not rob me of the job of living. She has an irrepressible spirit that yields to no adversity, and that part of her spirit that she shared with us was as fine a gift as any mother ever gave her children.

John McCain with Mark Salter, *Faith of My Fathers*, New York: Random House, 1999, p. 103.

the family cars, it was Roberta Wright McCain who made the family decisions.

Even when he was home, Jack McCain was not interested in shopping or making household decisions, so he was more than willing to let his wife do it. Though his name was on the checks, it was Roberta who wrote them. She admitted that she never even bothered to forge his signature, but rather signed his name in her own distinctive handwriting. "If Jack McCain ever paid a bill," she told people, "they'd send it back as a forgery."[9]

His Mother's Mobile Classroom

His mother also felt strongly that the children would learn as much as they could as they traveled to keep up with their father. In fact, she viewed those cross-country trips to a new base as an opportunity to see what a great country they lived in. If the trip took a week longer because of their educational stops, Roberta McCain decided, that was just fine.

She planned out routes that would take them to see historical landmarks or an exciting museum or art exhibit. Whenever they passed through a city, she and the children searched for whatever the residents considered most noteworthy, and spent time there.

Even today, McCain remembers how impressive some of these places were. "I recall being greatly impressed with Carlsbad Caverns, the Grand Canyon, the Petrified Forest, the high bluffs and Civil War history of Natchez, Mississippi, and the venerated shrines of American heroes, especially Washington's Mount Vernon and Andrew Jackson's Hermitage," he says. "They were all memorable events in my childhood, and I recall them today with gratitude."[10]

A Limited Education

But while his mother's instructive road trips added a great deal to their education, the schooling the McCain children were receiving was far below average. This was due to the minimal schools provided by the navy bases where their father was stationed.

Most were little more than converted aircraft hangars that lacked even the basic supplies for a school. They were limited as to what they could teach children, not only because of the mixture of ages of the students in the room, but also because of the rapid turnover of teachers. "We might have one teacher on Monday and a different one on Tuesday," recalls McCain. "On other days, we lacked the services of any teacher at all."[11]

Jack and Roberta McCain were concerned about all three of the children, but Johnny was a special case. They had always wanted him follow in the footsteps of his father and grandfather, and attend the United States Naval Academy in Annapolis, Maryland, after high school. It was a family tradition; one that they were sure would be a good career for their son, just as it had been for the first two John Sidney McCains.

McCain's parents, Roberta and John S. McCain Jr., pictured in 1961, had high hopes that young John would attend the U.S. Naval Academy just as his father and grandfather had done.

But the academy had rigorous admission standards. A high grade point average was required, preferably one earned at a good school. If young Johnny McCain would have any chance of getting in, he needed to get a better education than the one he was getting at the navy bases to which his father was assigned. So in 1951, with the Naval Academy only three years away, it was necessary to put Johnny in a different sort of school. It was a boarding school in Alexandria, Virginia, called Episcopal High School. EHS, as it was known, had a good reputation for discipline and high educational standards. And though they would miss having their son around, Roberta and Jack McCain felt that it was the best they could do to ensure his future in the Naval Academy.

"You Might as Well Have Been on Parris Island"

Episcopal High School was far different than any school McCain had ever experienced. It was a very old school—in fact, it was the oldest high school in Virginia, and opened its doors in 1839. In 1951 EHS was all male, including its faculty. The student body of the school was homogenous in other ways, too—it was almost all made up of young men from the cream of southern high society. Few of them had ever met someone like McCain, who was a member of a career navy family.

EHS had very strict regulations, which were diligently enforced. Students were required to wear jackets and ties to classes. They were allowed extended trips off campus only three times each year. One Monday per month, students could leave the campus for a short time, but school officials checked on them, to make sure they were signed in at the appointed time. Students were required to attend chapel every morning, and church every Sunday. McCain's classmate Charles Hooff recalls, "You might as well have been on Parris Island [a South Carolina U.S. Marine boot camp]."[12]

While the school was focused on tradition and rules, there were no frills to the accommodations. In fact, as McCain's classmate Ken Ringle described it years later, EHS was a very dreary place:

> We lived in curtained alcoves; ... slept on sagging pipe-frame beds; drank milk drawn from some dairy where, it seemed, the cows grazed on nothing but onions, and amused ourselves at meals by covertly flipping butter pats with knives onto the ceiling, where they would later melt free to drop on other, unsuspecting skulls.[13]

"He Was Considered Kind of a Punk"

John McCain entered EHS, as he had often entered new places in his wandering childhood—with a chip on his shoulder. Short and thin like his father, he tended to compensate for his small stature by trying to present a tough-guy image. The best way to do that, McCain remembers, was to fight the first kid who provoked him, no matter how big that kid was:

> Whether or not I lost those fights wasn't as important as establishing myself as someone who could adapt to the challenges of a new environment without betraying apprehension. I foolishly believed that fighting, as well as challenging school authorities and ignoring school regulations, was indispensable to my self-esteem and helped me form new friendships.[14]

Most of his EHS schoolmates felt McCain was unlikable right from the start. He projected a tough image, and seemed ready to fight almost constantly. One classmate, Rives Richey, became one of McCain's best friends in high school. Richey remembers McCain as very different from his other classmates, and agrees that he was not well-liked by most of them. "He was considered kind of a punk,"[15] says Richey. Indeed, his reputation resulted in two often-used nicknames: Punk and McNasty.

While a student at Episcopal High School, John McCain was known for his messy, unkempt appearance; a long way from the polished, clean look he maintained while attending the U.S. Naval Academy, as shown here.

Worst Rat

McCain's attitude was fueled by the rules at Episcopal High School, too. Interestingly, the school's many rules were not enforced as much by teachers and staff, but by upperclassmen. In a form of initiation, called hazing, known as the "Rat System," older students had almost total control over the school's newest students.

Every first-year student was considered a rat. That meant he was completely at the mercy of upperclassmen. What would perhaps seem abusive in other settings was normal for first-years at EHS. The intimidation was usually emotional, rather than physical. Rats were required to obey orders of the older students, and if they were slow or disrespectful, they were chastised and given harsh punishments.

McCain resented the system. He disliked having to comply with ridiculous requests from upperclassmen, and often refused. As a result, the older boys resented him. "I was one of the smaller boys in my class, a fact that upperclassmen, annoyed by my obdurate refusal to show a rat's humility, took to be further evidence of arrogance on my part,"[16] he recalls. At the end of his first year, McCain was voted "worst rat," which he considered a badge of honor.

The Nonconformist

One of the ways he showed his disdain for school rules was to bend the dress code. He wore the rattiest jacket and tie he could find, along with a dirty pair of blue jeans. His jeans were legendary; a half-century later, his classmates still recall them.

"John used to wear his jeans day in and day out," says his friend Rives Richey, "week in and week out to where they would almost stand up in the corner by themselves. And a lot of people thought maybe he should have washed a little more or something. His blue jeans would be just filthy."[17]

One of his teachers recalls that the rest of his clothing were much, either. "His coat would be something the Salvation Army would have rejected," he says. "And his shoes would be held together with tape."[18]

Finding a Niche

While he resented much about the high school as he was cultivating his bad-boy image, McCain still managed to find a group of friends that he enjoyed. The school encouraged athletics, and he played football, tennis, and joined the wrestling team. "I wasn't an exceptional athlete," he remembers, "but I was good enough to earn the respect of my teammates and coaches."[19]

His wrestling coach, Riley Deeble, agrees. He says that McCain and his friend Rives Richey both were small, tough, and cocky, competing together in the 127-pound class. "Maybe Napoleon was like that when he was young," says Deeble. "But a lot of people who are small physically do seem to, certainly in the school atmosphere, become a little extra aggressive to make up for it. They create a little more space around themselves so they don't get stepped on."[20]

But what won the most admiration of the boys in his small group of friends was his nonconformity. He seemed to do what he wanted, when he wanted to do it. He also seemed to be able to leave the school grounds whenever he had a notion to—whether it was to smoke (forbidden at EHS)—or to head to nearby Washington, D.C., to drink beer.

Ken Ringle recalls that seeing his friend in a coat was a sign he was leaving campus to smoke. "The one way to do the illegal smoking was to sneak off into the woods," says Ringle. "His coat was a sign that he was always skipping off, because in the winter it was cold out there. McCain also skipped off into Washington where he would go to places and drink occasionally. ... Beer was a forbidden thrill."[21]

"I Worshipped Him"

One of the few bright spots at Episcopal High School was his relationship with one of the teachers, William Ravenel. McCain had always loved reading, but Ravenel's classes gave him a new appreciation for English literature that he never had before—especially the plays of Shakespeare.

One of John McCain's favorite high school teachers, William Ravenel, had been part of General George Patton's (pictured) legendary tank corps during World War II.

But in addition to being a compelling and motivating English teacher, Ravenel coached the junior varsity football team, on which McCain played. Ravenel was also a soldier, having been part of General George S. Patton's legendary tank corps during World War II. He continued to serve in the army reserve while he taught at EHS.

Ravenel had the ability to be genuinely interested in his students. McCain found him an inspiration—someone who really understood him. "I worshipped him," McCain says. "He saw something in me that others did not. And he took a very personal interest in me and we spent a good deal of time together. He had a very important influence on my life."[22]

"The Only Person... I Wanted to See"

Interestingly, it was because of McCain's constant misbehavior during his high school years that forged a special bond with Ravenel. When boys received demerits, the punishments were either to march for long periods of time around the school's long circular drive or to do yard work for one of the teachers. Luckily, McCain says, he was assigned to work in Mr. Ravenel's yard.

The young McCain found that he began to look forward to the extra work, for it gave him time to talk to the teacher. They talked about everything—from modern short stories to sports and from Ravenel's experiences in combat to McCain's own future at the Naval Academy. Ravenel was one of the few people at EHS to whom he disclosed his nervousness about following the path his family had set for him in the navy.

His bond with the teacher was so strong, in fact, that years later, after finally being released after five years in a North Vietnamese prison, his former teacher and friend was someone he needed to see. "Mr. Ravenel was the only person outside of my family whom I wanted to see," McCain remembers. "I felt he was someone to whom I could explain what had happened to me, and who would understand."[23]

He was never able to do that, however. Ravenel died of a heart attack just two years before McCain was released from the prison. The regret is something McCain says still haunts him.

Leaving EHS

McCain's grades in high school had never been good, for he did not put in enough work in most of his classes to receive high marks. English and history were interesting, but math and science bored him. His friends at EHS say they were astonished when, near the end of their senior year, the fun-loving daredevil they knew as Punk McCain mentioned that he was planning on attending the Naval Academy the following year.

"You know, frankly, honest to goodness, if they'd have rated everybody in the class for most likely to succeed," says Rives Richey, "I guarantee you, he'd have been in the bottom tenth, without any question."[24]

But as marginal as his behavior and grades had been, EHS had prepared him, at least, for the academy's entrance exams. McCain did well on the exams, received his acceptance, and was indeed bound for the Naval Academy. But as his father drove him to Annapolis one morning in June 1954, he was dreading it.

Chapter 2

To the Navy

Seventeen-year-old John McCain was not happy about his enrollment at the Naval Academy. The biggest reason was that he had no choice in the matter. "I was basically told when I was young," he told biographer Paul Alexander, "that I was going to the Naval Academy."[25]

McCain is quick to point out that he was never actually ordered to attend the academy and to pursue a navy career. Instead, he says, it was just assumed, because of his father's and grandfather's long, successful careers as navy men:

My father and grandfather believed they had discovered the perfect life for a man. To them, the Navy was the most accommodating profession for good men who craved adventure. They never imagined possessing a greater treasure than a life at sea, and they regarded it as a legacy they were proud to bestow on their descendants, who, they assumed, would be appropriately grateful.[26]

Easing in

The summer before classes began, all first year students (called "plebes") arrived on the campus. There were more than twelve hundred of them, and they would receive their first training by some junior officers and a select group of upperclassmen. McCain, who had been positively dreading his arrival on campus, was surprised. He actually found those first weeks pleasant.

The days were spent learning to march in formation, getting to know his classmates, and playing sports. He was introduced to boxing and loved it. The cloud that had seemed to hover over him during high school began to disappear. His superiors, instead of being annoyed with him, believed McCain could make a good leader, and they made him company commander.

Those pleasant days came to an end, however. The day after Labor Day the rest of the school returned to campus, as McCain says, "eager to commence their campaign to humiliate, degrade, and make miserable me and every other plebe they encountered."[27]

Weeding out Plebes

If McCain thought that the rules and regulations at Episcopal High School were strict, he could find no words to adequately describe those at the Naval Academy. Plebe year was undoubtedly the worst, and it was meant to be. The idea was to weed out those who could not take the pressure, the constant yelling, the insistence on perfection from teachers and upperclassmen.

Just as John McCain had done in 1954, a first year cadet at the U.S. Naval Academy, or "plebe," gets his hair cut during Introduction Day in 2003.

Some of the conditions under which plebes had to function are listed by military expert John Karagaac:

> The plebe will be barked at, shouted at, forced to memorize at all times. He will be forced to stand in that demeaning and exaggerated attention known as 'the brace.'… The plebe will grow accustomed to the timetable, punctuated by bells, that dominates his whole existence; he will grow accustomed to drill and marching and quickly eating in the cavernous mess hall; he will, by degrees, accommodate himself to the constant inspection of room and uniform—aggressive, probing, minute inspection.[28]

Those who could not function in such conditions would not make good navy officers, and it was better that they found that out sooner, rather than later. Though the process was unpleasant, it was effective. More than 25 percent of the class would quit by senior year—either by choice, or because they were told that they did not meet navy standards.

Unrelenting Hazing

While McCain could have probably endured the school's rules, the hazing upset him. He and other first years had been forced to endure the abuse and ridicule by upperclassmen at EHS, but the hazing process at the Naval Academy was far worse. Plebes were forced to stand at attention anytime an upperclassman walked into the room. The older student could order a plebe to locate some trivial piece of information at the library, and recite it from memory. He would be asked to polish shoes, get up early and clean an upperclassman's room, or any other mindless task—without complaint. A plebe who could not perfectly complete the task—which was most likely what the upperclassman hoped would happen—was forced to endure punishments that were humiliating and degrading.

The menial and mind-numbing tasks and harsh punishments that older students set for the plebes were even worse when his father was at the academy a generation before. The usual tool for punishing a plebe for disrespect or for not doing one of the mindless tasks set out for him by older students was a broom with its bristles cut off just below the stitching.

One academy classmate of Jack McCain recalls his horror at seeing just how cruel that weapon was. "A man pulled that thing back as hard as he could, like a baseball bat," he recalled, "and whacked you with it when you were bent over. The first time it hit you, you just couldn't believe that a broom could do that. It jolted your backside right through the top of your head."[29]

Headstrong and Independent

McCain found the hazing repulsive. He made a decision to cooperate with those doing the hazing, but at the same time he let them know that he disliked them, and had nothing but resentment for what they were doing. "I wanted the lords of the first and second class [junior and seniors] to know my compliance was grudging," he says, "and in no way implied my respect for them."[30]

While at the Naval Academy, McCain found the harsh hazing of plebes many times went too far, and he stood up for underclassmen he thought were being mistreated.

A Natural Leader

"**P**eople kind of gravitated to him," says Chuck Larson, a classmate of McCain's at the Naval Academy. "They would respond to his lead. They pretty much cared about his approval and they cared about what he thought."

Another classmate, Jack Dittrick, found that quality mysterious. "Whatever John would suggest that we do, whether it was at the Academy or on liberty, I tended to follow," he said. "And I don't think I'm alone in that. I've talked with other classmates and we all marvel at how much control John had over what we did."

Quoted in Robert Timberg, *The Nightingale's Song*, New York: Simon & Schuster, 1995, pp. 33–34.

Sometimes, his outspoken nature impressed his peers. Early in his sophomore year, he and some friends were in the dining room when an upperclassman began verbally abusing a young Filipino who was a dining room worker. Other diners nearby, sensing that it was getting ugly, ate quickly and left, feeling embarrassed for the worker. But McCain could not leave without saying something, his roommates recalled later.

He said, "Hey Mister, why don't you pick on someone your own size?" The senior, annoyed that a younger student would dare to speak to him like that, demanded his name. "Midshipman McCain, third class," McCain replied. "What's yours?"[31] The enraged senior did not answer, and quickly left the dining room.

Frank Gamboa, one of McCain's former roommates, says that was typical of his friend. He hated when people used rank or social position to bully other people. That is why many of McCain's classmates looked up to him—he did the right thing without thinking twice about it. "Give me a couple of weeks to think about it," says Gamboa, "and I might have been that brave."[32]

"He Was There Because It Was the Family Business"

Though things improved after the constant hazing of plebe year, McCain was as headstrong and independent during the next three years at the academy. He broke as many rules there as he could get away with.

One friend from that time remembers thinking that McCain's attitude had a lot to do with the fact that he had no choice about where he went to school. Though he was very proud of his grandfather and father, McCain did not think he could ever measure up to their success. "He had a little bit of internal conflict," he says. "His legacy weighed heavy on him. I was there because I wanted to be. He was there because it was the family business."[33]

Whatever the reason, McCain kept his quarters messy, and his uniform was rarely as clean and pressed as it was supposed to be. He was sarcastic, usually late, and his grades were barely good enough to get by. As a result of such infractions, wrote the *Los Angeles Times* years later, "by the end of his sophomore year he had marched enough extra duty to go from Annapolis to Baltimore and back 17 times."[34]

A Visit from Dad

McCain says that even with his consistent misbehavior, he almost never heard from his father about his antics at the academy. However, one evening as he and his roommates were having a wild water balloon fight in their room, his father made a surprise visit. There was a knock at the door, and the roommate who answered was astonished to see an officer standing there.

The roommates all snapped to attention, but a stunned McCain merely said, "Dad?" It was Jack McCain, and giving a stern look to all of them, told his son to meet him downstairs in five minutes.

When he met his father a few minutes later, the elder McCain lectured his son on his behavior. "You're in too much trouble here, Johnny," he said, "to be asking for any more." Later, McCain wrote, "That single incident is the only time I can remember my father upbraiding me for my dismal performance as a midshipman."[35]

Fifth from the Bottom

His record in the classroom was disappointing, too. He did well in history and literature—two subjects he had always found interesting. Unfortunately for McCain, however, they

President Dwight D. Eisenhower hands out diplomas to the graduating Naval Academy class in 1958, of which John McCain was a member.

made up only a very small part of the course work in the Naval Academy. Most of the courses he found dull, and he rarely studied for tests.

His friends say that he tended to put off studying until the very last minute, and when he did, he often enlisted friends to help him understand particularly difficult parts of the course work. Remembers one friend, "He only wanted to know enough to get by."[36]

Even so, McCain managed to do just well enough to be able to graduate in June 1958—fifth from the bottom of his class. U.S. president Dwight D. Eisenhower delivered the graduation address and handed out diplomas to the graduates. Interestingly, thirty-five years later, in 1993, McCain himself was chosen to give the graduation address at the Naval Academy—a situation that he found very ironic. "America is a land of opportunity, where anything is possible," he told the graduates. "And my being given this honor proves it."[37]

Flight School

Although McCain was done with the academy, his education continued. McCain had decided to become a navy pilot. The idea of being a pilot was far more intriguing to him than serving on a battleship.

Attending flight school in Pensacola, Florida, was far more fun than the academy had been, too. He and his fellow students lived their own lives, and had no restrictions on their antics. Driving a new Corvette he had received after graduation, McCain enjoyed his independence—especially the freedom that came from no longer living in a Naval Academy dormitory. He dated a lot, played all-night poker with his friends, and generally had a great deal of fun.

He also surprised himself in that he enjoyed learning to be a pilot. McCain found that he loved the feeling of being in the air, of being apart from the restrictions that had bothered him about his other studies. An added bonus was that it was entirely unlike what his father had done in the navy. Being a flyer was a way for

Two Mistakes

McCain's crash when he was shot down over Hanoi was not the first time he had experienced plane trouble. Though he loved flying, he was not very good at it—at least, at first. In fact, he had had two other incidents in the years before he went to Vietnam. When practicing landings over Spain while in flight training, he flew too low and took out several power lines—which deprived part of the country of electricity for a time. In another practice run in Texas, he crashed his plane into Corpus Christi Bay. Though knocked out temporarily, he managed to get out of the cockpit before the plane sank.

him to continue the McCain navy tradition, yet still carve out his own niche, out of the shadow of his famous father.

Intense Training

For the next two years, McCain continued his pilot training. In addition to his training in Florida, he spent time in the Mediterranean Sea, flying planes from an aircraft carrier. He spent time in Corpus Christi, Texas, too. He also did time in the Caribbean Sea, when an international crisis arose in 1962 after the Soviet Union began basing nuclear missiles in Cuba—just ninety miles from U.S. soil. He and other pilots on the USS *Enterprise*, an aircraft carrier, were waiting for orders to bomb those Soviet bases. And although the crisis was resolved peacefully in less than a week, it made an impact on McCain. He began to look forward to using some of the skills he was learning—something he had never thought about before.

"We weren't disappointed to be denied our first combat experience," he wrote later, "but our appetites were whetted and our imaginations fueled. We eagerly anticipated the occasion when

McCain was stationed aboard the U.S.S. Enterprise,
pictured, during the Cuban Missile Crisis in 1962.

we would have the chance to do what we were trained to do, and discover, at last, if we were brave enough for the job."[38]

Thinking About Vietnam

The most obvious place to use that knowledge as a navy pilot was in Vietnam. Since the early 1960s, the United States had been sending troops to support the South Vietnamese in their fight against the Communist North Vietnamese. The Vietnam War was controversial in the United States, for many believed American troops did not belong there.

McCain was not concerned with the politics of the war, however. What he was interested in was becoming a better pilot. He was taking his job—and its responsibilities—seriously. He had been raised in a family where talk of wartime experiences was common. He writes that as a young boy, he would listen to his father and his friends reminisce about things that had happened during World War II:

> They talked about battles on sea and land, kamikaze attacks, depth-charge attacks, Marine landings on fiercely defended Pacific atolls, submerged battles between submarines, gun battles between ships of the line—all the drama and fury of war that most kids went to the movies to experience.[39]

Perhaps, he thought, it was his turn to become a leader, to have wartime experiences and prove himself. He requested a combat tour in Vietnam. McCain realized that this was certainly a dramatic change from the party-boy who had slouched through the Naval Academy, but he felt he was ready.

The End of the Bachelor Life

Another aspect of McCain's life had changed as well. While he was stationed in Pensacola, he had renewed a friendship with a young woman named Carol Shepp. He had known her during his days at the Naval Academy, when she was dating a classmate.

John McCain and Carol Shepp, pictured in 1973, were married in 1965.

A former fashion model from Philadelphia, Pennsylvania, she had married the classmate, but after several years was the divorced mother of two small boys.

Shepp had been visiting a friend in Pensacola, when she ran into McCain. The two began dating soon afterwards. He remembered later how attractive and smart she was, and her kindness was endearing. He was surprised and happy that she seemed to be as attracted to him as he was to her. By the time he transferred to Meridian, Mississippi, to begin training young pilots, McCain was flying up to Philadelphia almost every weekend to see her and the boys—Douglas and Andrew.

Less than a year later, McCain came to what was, for him, quite a startling realization. He wanted to give up his bachelor life. He had found someone with whom he wanted to spend the rest of his life. The two were married in July 1965. A year later, he adopted the two boys, and a few months after that their daughter Sidney Ann McCain was born.

Just months after the birth of his first child, McCain received new orders. He was assigned to a squadron scheduled to head to Vietnam in the summer of 1967. This was what he wanted, but as he completed last-minute training at a Mississippi airfield in the months before he left, he wondered whether or not he was ready.

Chapter 3

Service in Vietnam

McCain's first combat assignment was aboard an aircraft carrier called the USS *Forrestal*. In the summer of 1967, the *Forrestal* was working in the South China Sea, about sixty miles from the coast of North Vietnam. Each day planes took off from its four acres of deck space for bombing missions against North Vietnamese targets.

A Day Like Any Other

For the pilots and crew on the *Forrestal*, July 29, 1967, started off like any other. McCain and the other pilots were getting ready to take off on their missions. They usually left about 11:00 A.M. McCain flew an attack plane called a Skyhawk. Laden with 500- or 1,000-pound bombs, the Skyhawks had a second gas tank that held an extra 200 gallons of aviation gas. This made it possible to go further inland in their bombing assignments.

Also on the deck was a second type of plane, the Phantoms. These were special planes that protected the Skyhawks. They were armed with powerful Zuni rockets that could be fired at any enemy aircraft trying to take down the bombers.

As McCain sat in his Skyhawk, he went through his preflight checks, making certain that everything was in working order on the plane. Like every other pilot, he was a creature of routines—almost superstitions—that made him calmer before each mission. They were aware that American planes were being shot down regularly, and dozens of pilots had already been captured or killed. The routines gave them something to focus on before takeoff, other than the frightening possibilities.

The last thing McCain did each time was to hand his helmet down to crewman Tom Ott, who would clean off the plastic visor before each mission. "Tom had heard me complain that I often found it difficult to see through my visor," McCain says. "So he always came on deck before launch to clean it one more time."[40]

Nightmare at Sea

After cleaning the helmet, Ott signaled good luck to McCain, flashing him a thumbs-up. McCain shut his canopy—the top of the cockpit—and within a few seconds, it seemed the world had exploded. A plane starting up had sent a burst of flame, which ignited one of the Zuni rockets on a nearby Phantom. The rocket had screamed across the *Forrestal's* deck, hitting McCain's plane—setting his extra fuel tank on fire.

John McCain was waiting to take off from the deck of the U.S.S Forrestal *when a stray rocket hit his plane causing the gas tank to explode. McCain managed to escape, but 134 crew members were killed in the ensuing explosions and fire.*

Within seconds, fire had consumed the aircraft carrier's deck. As fireballs of highly flammable aviation gas flew along the deck to other planes, they caused bombs on those planes to explode and more Zuni rockets to ignite.

McCain opened his canopy and crawled out onto the nose of his plane, where he jumped down into the inferno. He quickly rolled to extinguish the flames on his clothing, and got a close look at the nightmare that had taken over the *Forrestal:*

> All around me was mayhem. Planes were burning. More bombs cooked off. Body parts, pieces of the ship, and scraps of planes were dropping onto the deck. Pilots strapped in their seats ejected into the firestorm. Men trapped by flames jumped overboard. More Zuni missiles streaked across the deck. Explosions tore craters in the flight deck, and burning fuel fell through the openings into the hangar bay, spreading the fire below.[41]

To the *Oriskany*

It looked for a time as though the *Forrestal* might sink as the fire continued to spread. Frantic crew members worked to push unexploded bombs and planes into the sea before they, too, could explode and cause more damage. For more than a day, the fire burned. When it was finally brought under control, the extent of the damage was evident.

More than twenty planes had been destroyed. More importantly, 134 men were dead or dying—most from burns. Dozens more were injured.

Amazingly, the *Forrestal* was not destroyed, but the repairs would take a long time. After the ship made its way slowly to a nearby naval base in the Philippines, pilots were given a chance to transfer to another aircraft carrier. One possibility was a carrier called the *Oriskany.* A number of its pilots had been shot down as they did their bombing missions, and they were looking for new pilots to fill those spots. McCain volunteered, and in September 1967 his orders took him to the *Oriskany.* Although

The Voice

Though he made many friends during his years as a prisoner of war, McCain grew closer to Bob Craner than any other—even though for a very long time, they could not see one another.

"McCain and I leaned on each other a great deal," Craner later said. "We were separated by about eighteen inches of brick, and I never saw the guy for the longest time. I used to have dreams. . . we all did, of course, and they were sometimes nightmares . . . and my world had shrunk to a point where the figures in my dreams were myself, the guards, and a voice . . . and that was McCain.

"I didn't know what he looked like, so I could not visualize him in my dreams, because he became the guy—the only guy—I turned to, for a period of two years. . . . We opened up and talked about damn near everything besides our immediate problems—past life, and all the family things we never would have talked to anybody about. We derived a great deal of strength from this."

Quoted in John McCain with Mark Salter, *Faith of My Fathers*, New York: Random House, 1999, p. 230.

he had no way of knowing it at the time, it would be his last combat assignment.

"I'm Hit"

October 26, 1967, was the day of his twenty-third bombing mission—almost three months to the day after the *Forrestal* fire. McCain was one of twenty Skyhawk pilots that were to bomb a large power plant located in Hanoi, the largest city in North Vietnam. It was an especially dangerous mission, since Hanoi was

An American warplane is shot down and the pilot ejects north of Hanoi, Vietnam in 1966. While flying a mission in the same area in 1967, McCain's plane was shot down and he was taken prisoner by the North Vietnamese.

heavily defended against the possibility of air strikes. He would have to drop his bombs on the power plant and quickly get out of the area before the deadly surface-to-air missiles, known as SAMs, could shoot his plane out of the sky.

As he flew closer to his target, McCain saw his instrument panel begin lighting up, warning him of the SAMs trying to lock onto his position. He dove down to 4,500 feet and dropped the bombs, when another warning sounded. Suddenly, a SAM the size and shape of a telephone pole seemed to come out of nowhere, and ripped the right wing off the Skyhawk.

McCain recalled later that he did not feel the paralyzing sense of panic one might expect in such a situation. As his plane went into a nose dive towards the ground, he writes in his memoir entitled *Faith of My Fathers*, his pilot's training took over:

> I didn't feel fear or any more excitement than I had already experienced during the run, my adrenaline surging as I dodged SAMs and flak [antiaircraft fire from the ground] to reach the target. I didn't think, 'Gee, I'm hit—what now?' I reacted automatically the moment I took the hit and saw that my wing was gone. I radioed, 'I'm hit,' reached up, and pulled the ejection seat handle.[42]

"My God—My Leg!"

The moment he ejected, he was knocked unconscious. The force of the ejection had knocked his helmet and oxygen mask off. It had also rammed his body into the instrument panel, which broke his left knee and both arms. He came to as he hit the water of Truc Bach Lake below. The lake, located in the center of the city, was only twenty feet deep, but it might as well have been ten times that depth, for he was unable to swim. Not only was he weighed down with fifty pounds of equipment and protective gear, but he could not move his arms to tread water. As the force of his fall took him to the bottom of the lake, he managed to kick up with his good leg, only to sink down again.

John McCain is pulled out of Truc Bach Lake after being shot down by North Vietnamese surface-to-air missiles on October 26, 1967.

Dazed and confused as to why he could not move his arms, he tried to use his teeth to inflate the life preserver strapped to his chest. Finally he was able to bite down on the switch and pulled, and suddenly he floated back to the surface. The first thing he saw was a crowd of North Vietnamese civilians that had gathered on the shore.

A few of them swam out to bring McCain to shore. As he was hauled onto the shore by the rest of the onlookers, he watched helplessly as they stripped off his clothes and began spitting at him and kicking him. What alarmed him more, however, was the sight of his leg. His knee had been broken, and his leg lay uselessly at a frighteningly unnatural angle—his right foot resting next to his right knee. He cried out, "My God—my leg!"[43]

His alarm seemed to enrage the crowd. Someone smashed a rifle butt into his shoulder, breaking it. Someone else stuck a bayonet in his ankle and groin. As he lay in agony, helpless against the angry Vietnamese citizens, an enemy army truck pulled up and loaded him on a stretcher. He was taken a few blocks away, to a prison that POWs (prisoners of war) referred to as the "Hanoi Hilton." Things, he knew, were about to get much, much worse.

Interrogation

McCain was taken on the stretcher to a cell. He was wet, still in his underwear, but his captors had thrown a blanket over him. For the next few days, he was in and out of consciousness, but received no medical treatment for his wounds. During the times he was awake, he was taken to another room to be interrogated. North Vietnamese officials wanted to know what his mission had been, and what other missions were being planned by the Americans.

As he had been trained, McCain gave his interrogators nothing except his name, rank, and military serial number. When he would not answer their questions, they would hit him. "I was in such bad shape," he remembers, "that every time they hit me, it would knock me unconscious. They kept saying, 'You will not receive any medical treatment until you talk.'" [44]

McCain did not believe them, however. He believed that if he held out long enough, they would take him to the hospital. His lapses in and out of consciousness, he later realized, were a blessing, because unconsciousness allowed him to escape the pain of his broken limbs. But on the fourth day, something happened that really frightened him.

Too Late

Two guards came into his cell. One lifted the blanket from their prisoner's leg, and showed the other McCain's wounds. It was then that McCain saw his knee. It had swollen to the size of a football, and had turned a frightening reddish-brown. He had heard of another soldier who had experienced such an injury—and had not survived:

I remembered that when I was a flying instructor, a fellow had ejected from his plane and broken his thigh. He had gone into shock, the blood had pooled in his leg, and he died, which came as quite a surprise to us—a man dying of a broken leg. Then I realized that a very similar thing was happening to me.[45]

Realizing that he had to do something, McCain told the guard to get the officer who had been interrogating him. The officer, known as "The Bug" to prisoners, had one eye that looked sideways, and another that was clouded with a white cataract. When the Bug came into his cell, McCain told him that he would talk if he could be taken to a hospital.

The Bug brought a prison doctor to McCain's cell. The doctor took McCain's pulse and examined his leg, and spoke quickly to the Bug. Impatient, McCain asked when he could get treatment. But the Bug told him he would get no treatment, for the doctor had determined that he would not survive. It was too late, Bug told McCain.

A High-Profile Prisoner of War

McCain was terrified. It seemed they were leaving him to die in his cell. There was nothing he could do; he was completely at the mercy of his captors. As he became more and more discouraged, the Bug suddenly came rushing back into the cell, announcing excitedly that McCain was the grandson of a famous admiral. In the Bug's mind, this meant that McCain was important and famous, too.

This was very good news for the North Vietnamese. Anytime they had a high-profile prisoner of war—either one of very high rank, or else someone from an important family—it gave them a propaganda tool. They would take good care of that prisoner and then have him publicly denounce his own country. At the same time, he would be told to praise his captors, telling the world how well they treated their prisoners of war.

McCain did not think about any of that. All he knew was that he finally was going to the hospital. And while the hospital room

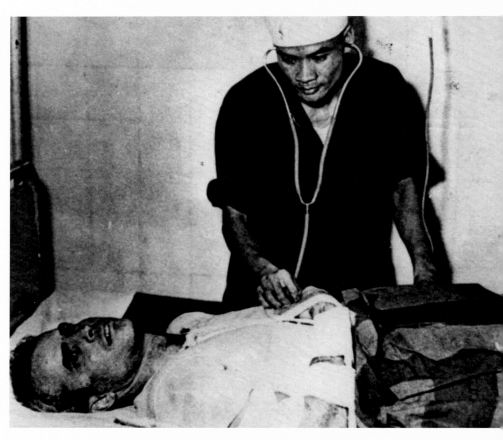

Only after his captors learned that McCain was the grandson of a famous admiral did they finally take him to a hospital. Here, McCain is being examined in a Hanoi hospital.

was infested with rats and was crawling with roaches, he was happy. Doctors had begun giving him IVs of blood and nutrients. He was in a bed and he was going to get well.

Demands

While in the hospital, doctors tried to set his fractured right arm, but the attempt—all done on a wide-awake McCain, without anesthetic—was a failure. The arm was broken in three places,

"I Told Over a Hundred Movies"

With no reading material or other form of entertainment, POWs found more resourceful ways to pass the time when they were not in solitary.

"One of our most popular entertainments . . . were our productions of Sunday, Wednesday, and Saturday Nights at the movies," recalls McCain. "I told over a hundred movies in prison, some of them many times over. I tried to recall every movie I had ever seen, from *Stalag 17* to *One-Eyed Jacks* (a camp favorite).

"Often running short of popular fare, I would make up movies I had never seen. Pilots shot down during air raids in 1972 were a valuable resource for me. They had seen movies that I had not. Desperate for new material, I would pester them almost as soon as they arrived and before they had adjusted to their new circumstances. 'What movies have you seen lately? Tell me about them.' . . . They probably thought prison life had seriously affected my mind."

John McCain with Mark Salter, *Faith of My Fathers*, New York: Random House, 1999, p. 330.

and the doctors could not get them to line up properly. In the end, they simply put a large cast that went from his waist to his neck.

McCain was then moved to a cleaner, brighter room to be interviewed by a French journalist. The prison officials wanted McCain to condemn his own actions, and those of his country. He gave fairly brief answers to the journalist's questions, but no more details about his war activities than he had supplied to his interrogators.

Although the North Vietnamese stood nearby during the interview and urged him to condemn the United States for their role in the war, he would not do it. As a result, after the interview was over, McCain was beaten. The inhumane treatment he received would continue over the next five years.

"You Need to Put Me with Some Americans"

Despite his six-week hospital stay, McCain did not get better. He had constant diarrhea, stomach cramps so severe he could not eat. He was in agony from his broken limbs. The prison doctors said that not only was he not improving, but he was getting much worse. McCain offered a solution. "You need to put me with some Americans," he told one prison official, "because I'm not going to get better here."[46] Blindfolded later that night, he was taken in an army truck to another prison, where he would have two roommates—Bud Day, an air force pilot, and Norris Overly, an air force officer.

Day and Overly were shocked at the appearance of the new arrival. He was little more than a skeleton, and his prematurely gray hair was pure white. He was covered with boils and infected sores, recalls Day, and they were convinced he would be dead within a day or two:

> When they brought John in, I'd say he probably weighed around 100 pounds. He was just horribly skinny. He was in the huge cast that was wearing a hole in his elbow. He was really very tender. … He was also filthy. He hadn't been washed, I don't think, since he had been shot down. He had a bunch of food in his hair, and a beard, and he just smelled like he was rotten.[47]

The two men began caring for McCain. They helped him eat, which he could not do alone because of his broken arms. They helped him use the toilet (really, a rusted bucket in the corner of the cell), which he had not been able to do up until then, either. "You know," says Day, "he couldn't do the first thing for himself."[48]

The Breaking Point

McCain began to heal under his cellmates' care—so much so that after a few months, prison officials deemed him healthy enough to return to solitary. He was also healthy enough, it seemed, to be beaten and tortured.

John McCain as he looked in a POW mug shot taken by the North Vietnamese sometime between 1967 and 1973.

Officials told him that they had decided to allow him to be released from prison. All he would have to do, they explained, was to sign a letter admitting that he was a war criminal and denouncing the United States. Although he would have loved nothing more than to return home, he knew that it would be a violation of the prisoner of war (POW) code of conduct. Prisoners were released in the order in which they had been captured. Leaving before men who had been imprisoned years longer than McCain would be wrong and unfair.

When he gave them his answer, he was tortured. Guards came into his cell and brutally beat him. As he lay on the floor, they kicked his ribs, his broken arms, and even his teeth. Every two or three hours, the guards would come back and repeat the same thing again. He held out for three days. But on the fourth day, he could take no more. He had several teeth broken off at the gum line. His ribs were broken, his arms and legs were bloody and broken. He wrote out the confession and signed it. "I am a black criminal," it read, "and I have performed deeds of an air pirate. I almost died, and the Vietnamese people saved my life, thanks to the doctors. ..."[49]

"I Was Ashamed"

McCain struggled with what had happened for years afterward—even after he and the other POWs came home in 1973. But the two weeks after his forced confession were the worst. He was sick with shame. At first he told himself he had held out longer than some prisoners, but that did not make him feel any better. "They were the worst two weeks of my life," he wrote later. "I couldn't rationalize away my confession. I was ashamed. I felt faithless, and I couldn't control my despair. I shook, as if my disgrace were a fever."[50]

Other prisoners he came into contact with told him that every prisoner had a breaking point. They reminded him that he did not take an early release, and urged him not to be so hard on himself. The support of his fellow POWs helped him put the episode into perspective. "I'm convinced that I did the best I could," he said years later, "but the best that I could wasn't good enough."[51]

Coming Home

When the war ended in 1973, the POWs came home in shifts. McCain's shift flew from Hanoi on an air force jet on March 14, 1973. He remembers being very happy, yet a little sad, too. He would be leaving POWs that he had come to consider as brothers. "The sudden separation hurt a little," he wrote later, "and on the

John McCain walks to freedom in Hanoi after being released from a Vietnamese POW camp on March 14, 1973.

flight home a strange sense of loneliness nagged me even as my excitement to see my family became more intense."[52]

It would be a long time before any of the POWs could put Vietnam behind them. The violence, the torture, and the loneliness for their families had been a way of life. And though they were glad to be heading home, it was a strange feeling—almost as if home was something unfamiliar.

Chapter 4

Beginning a New Life

The POWs returning home had a mixed welcome. The Vietnam War had divided the American people. Though some still supported it, a growing number were strongly opposed to it. Though many soldiers had been drafted and had no choice in going to Vietnam, some Americans blamed the returning soldiers for the U.S. government's unpopular war.

McCain and the other POWs, however, were warmly received by President Richard Nixon. The president held a reception a few months after their return. There is a famous photograph of John McCain, thin in his dress white uniform, leaning forward on crutches to shake hands with the smiling president. One POW recalls that Nixon had been a gracious host:

> We had the run of the White House. They even let people on the second floor. I mean, Nixon was . . . just bubbling. And he said, 'You want to go up and see the living quarters? Go ahead.' The Secret Service had a conniption, but he was the boss. So we went up.[53]

Now What?

McCain was excited to reconnect with his family. But once the initial excitement passed, he became concerned about what he was going to do with himself. His whole life had been about

John McCain is greeted by President Richard Nixon (left) during the presidential reception held in honor of the American prisoners of war, September 14, 1973.

the navy, and though as a young man he had resented the fact he had no choice in the matter, it was all he knew. Besides, before his plane had been shot down, he had grown to love flying.

But the John McCain of 1973 was in no condition to fly. Physically he was a wreck. His arms were virtually useless—he could not tie his shoes or comb his hair. One of his shoulder sockets had been crushed by a rifle butt during one of his many beatings. However, the damage that most worried McCain was that to his knee. Though he could not raise his arms, he could still operate the controls of a plane. His knee however was completely immobile and could not bend at all. He knew the navy would not allow him to return to flight status with his knee in this condition.

After spending a few weeks with Carol and his children, he checked into the naval hospital in Jacksonville, Florida. Doctors decided there was little they could do about his arms, but they performed two operations on his knee. They scraped scar tissue from the bones, hoping to increase the joint's mobility.

"The Pain Method"

After three months of hospitalization and therapy, he could only move his knee 10 degrees. It looked as though his flying days were over. Frustrated, McCain considered his options. He was thirty-six years old and had no idea what he could do with his life. He knew the navy would be glad to give him some administrative job, but he had no interest in sitting at a desk all day. As he became more and more gloomy, he received a very unusual telephone call—one that changed everything.

The call came from a physical therapist named Diane Rauch. She told McCain that she had heard of his case, and felt that she could help. She offered to work with him to get his knee more flexible, so that he could resume flying, and she would do it for free.

For the next year, Rauch worked on his knee. In what he called "the pain method,"[54] she had him sit for thirty minutes in a whirlpool, and then she would physically force his knee to bend, pushing as hard as she could until he could stand the pain no longer. Though the pain was terrible and the progress slow, by the end of a year he could bend his knee an unbelievable 90 degrees. He could qualify—just barely—to fly again.

Success and Failure

He was assigned as head of the Replacement Air Group (RAG) at an airfield in Jacksonville. Among other responsibilities, he trained pilots and crew who would later be assigned to aircraft carriers. He was thrilled with the work, and the young pilots were equally thrilled to be learning from him. "Everyone knew what McCain and the other POWs had been through over [in Vietnam]," recalls Chuck Nash, who did his training under McCain. "We all knew. To us, they were heroes. They were gods."[55]

His work as commander of the RAG was an unqualified success. Ironically, however, the same could not be said for his personal life. It was during this time that his marriage to Carol fell apart. He had a number of extramarital affairs, and Carol was devastated.

Though at first he explained the split as an effect of two people growing apart after so many years of being separated during the war, he later became more candid about his behavior. "My marriage's collapse was attributable to my own selfishness and immaturity more than it was to Vietnam, and I cannot escape blame by pointing a finger at the war. The blame was entirely mine."[56]

Senate Liaison

In early 1977, after his assignment with the RAG was over, McCain took a job unlike any navy position he had ever had before. He was assigned to the Senate as a navy liaison. Liaisons are go-betweens, making sure that correct information is exchanged between lawmakers and the military. Liaisons also act as escorts when congressional delegations go on overseas trips. For McCain, the job opened up a whole new world.

John McCain and his second wife, Cindy, on their wedding day, May 17, 1980.

He was a likable and engaging man, and he loved talking to people. And while many military liaisons before him had blended into the background in the Senate, McCain quickly achieved popularity among the lawmakers. It was to McCain's little office that many senators and staffers came at the end of a day to unwind and talk, and they thoroughly enjoyed his company. As one fellow liaison observed, "John McCain, as a Navy captain, knew on a personal basis more senators and was more warmly viewed than virtually any lobbyist I have ever known in this town; they loved to see him."[57]

It was during this new assignment that McCain fell in love again. While he was escorting a Senate delegation to China in late 1979, the group had a stopover for a military briefing in Hawaii. It was there that he met a twenty-five-year-old Arizona teacher named Cindy Hensley, on vacation with her parents. Though she was seventeen years younger than McCain, the two got along very well. "By the evening's end," he later recalled, "I was in love."[58] Within six months, in May 1980, the two were married.

A New Direction

Besides his marriage, the most important outcomes of this assignment was that it made McCain more aware of how things in Washington get done—or, in some cases, do not get done. He saw the complex maneuvering it takes for lawmakers to pass bills. He also realized that he could make a real difference by becoming a part of this process. Though the McCain tradition of service had always been military, he believed he was ready to carve out a new path.

In early 1981, McCain met with a political consultant named Jay Smith for advice on how to go about getting into politics. McCain explained that he planned to retire from the navy and run for office in the state of Arizona. Although McCain had higher aspirations, he wanted to start out as a congressional representative from Arizona.

The consultant later remembered the conversation as being very strange. Because of the long and difficult process of running a campaign for Congress, he assumed McCain was talking about running in 1984. No, McCain told him—he planned on running in the 1982 election. And when he asked McCain in what congressional district he would run, McCain was not sure yet. "I was astounded,"[59] Smith laughingly recalled saying.

Starting Slowly

The first step for McCain, Smith advised, was to get involved in Arizona state politics on a local level. It would be important to build up a strong political base. To do that, he needed to get to know various Republican leaders from Arizona. But, McCain later remembered, while this advice was probably wise, it sounded like

McCain holds a photo of a marker at Truc Bach Lake in Hanoi where he parachuted after being shot down as a navy pilot.

A Superstitious Moviegoer

John McCain enjoys campaigning, but the elections themselves are excruciating for him. He found that the only way he could calm down once his part of the campaign is through is to go to the movies. On election day in 1982, he went by himself to see *Star Wars*. On election day in 1988, when he ran for the Senate for the first time, he decided that the movie idea had been good luck, so he went to see *Crocodile Dundee*.

far too slow a process. "I had neither the time nor the patience to follow a ten-year plan for election to Congress," he writes in his memoir, *Worth the Fighting For*. "I was in my forties and in a hurry, ambitious for the kind of influence I had seen wielded by the country's most accomplished politicians, and worried that my chances were diminishing by the day."[60]

Even though he was impatient, he did what Smith suggested. After he and Cindy settled in Arizona, he got involved with state and local politics. He helped with fundraising and was booked as a speaker for local service clubs, telling about his experiences in Vietnam and in Washington, D.C. Cindy's father, a wealthy beer distributor in Arizona, hired McCain to do public relations work, so that he could build up contacts when he traveled to conventions around the state.

In 1982, just ten months before the election, a thirty-year congressman from Arizona's First District named John Rhodes announced that he was retiring. His seat would be open, and McCain knew that was his chance. The same day, he and his wife bought a house in the First District, which was part of Phoenix (it is a rule that a congressional representative must live in the district he or she represents). And excitedly, McCain began planning how he, who had never run for anything in his life, would go about winning a seat in the U.S. Congress.

"The Super Bowl of All Campaigns"

If Smith thought McCain was impatient before Rhodes resigned, he was almost unmanageable in the weeks afterwards. McCain wanted to declare his candidacy for the First District seat immediately. Because of his "let's hurry up and get out there" attitude, his friends began calling him The White Tornado. When he finally got the go-ahead from his political consultant to officially declare that he was running, McCain threw himself into the campaign with all his energy. Political consultant Jay Smith called it "the Super Bowl of all campaigns."[61]

One of the least-favorite campaign activities of most politicians is knocking on doors and introducing themselves to voters. But McCain embraced it. In fact, he set a goal for himself of knocking on as many doors as he possibly could between the start of his campaign and election day. He knocked on thousands of doors in Phoenix heat that often hovered around 102 degrees. From his miles and miles of walking, he wore out three pairs of shoes—the last of which his wife had bronzed as a souvenir. And every home he visited, he tried to connect with a voter.

"Listen, Pal"

Few knew who he was in the early weeks of the campaign. But as the months wore on, he found that he was becoming recognizable. People recognized his white hair, even if they could not remember his name. One day he realized that fewer people were coming to the door asking what he was selling, and more were listening to him talk about running for Congress.

The only issue that plagued him was the accusation that he was a carpetbagger—a derogatory term for someone moving to a region purely for personal gain. His opponents, who had all lived many years in Arizona, used the issue against him. They hoped that Arizona citizens would not consider voting for an outsider—a man who had never set foot in Arizona, one who had bought a house in the district the day the seat opened up.

After being accused of not being a "real" citizen of Arizona by his opponents in the 1982 congressional election, McCain lost his temper defending himself during a press conference. He eventually won the election.

McCain answered the charge politely at first. He explained that as the son of a navy officer, he moved around constantly. When he married, he settled in Arizona—his wife's home state. But the accusations kept coming up, and one day, he finally lost his temper when a questioner brought up the issue again:

Listen, pal, I spent twenty-two years in the Navy. My father was in the Navy. My grandfather was in the Navy. We in the military service tend to move a lot. We have to live in all parts of the country, all parts of the world. I wish I could have had the luxury, like you, of growing up and living and spending my entire life in a nice place like the first district of Arizona, but I was doing other things. As a matter of fact, when I think about it now, the place I lived longest in my life was Hanoi.[62]

Looking back, McCain says that though he did not realize it at the moment, it was a great time to lose his temper. The audience and the questioner were stunned by his answer, but it was the right things to say. In fact, his answer had two good qualities: first, it was true and second, it emphasized his great sacrifice to the country as a prisoner of war. Though McCain had begun the race as a complete long shot, after that day no one was very surprised when he won the election.

Congressman McCain

McCain was delighted to have won, but he knew this was just the beginning of what he hoped would be a long, meaningful political career. After leaving the navy, he had set high goals for himself. He wanted to be an important voice in foreign relations, and to be a strong voice for men and women serving in uniform. He was especially passionate about making certain that American troops would not be sent into war unless the nation's leaders were serious about winning the war—something that had been lacking during the Vietnam War, he believed. "The Vietnam experience made me want to be involved more in public service," he once said, "and seeing things happen right."[63]

But he was a newcomer, and it was important to learn as much as he could about this new job. He knew it was also critical to become familiar with those issues that were important to the voters in Arizona, such as mining concerns, water rights, and Native American issues. So he threw himself into learning to be a good congressman, with the same energy he had brought to his campaign.

This energy was immediately obvious in the amount of time he spent on airplanes. He had promised the voters during the campaign that if elected, he would remain accessible to them. He would not remain in Washington for so long that he would forget what the people of Arizona expected of him. But no one expected him to be as accessible as he turned out to be. He flew back to Arizona almost every weekend—a long, 4,000-miles round-trip. And all weekend, he worked—meeting with constituents, holding town meetings, and speaking to whatever group wanted him. It was, some observed, as though he were running for office all over again.

Not Just a Predictable Vote

One thing that soon became apparent was that even though McCain was an inexperienced newcomer to Congress, he was not going to do what many newcomers did—vote with his party on every

In 1983, when President Ronald Reagan, pictured, needed congressional approval to keep a peacekeeping force in Lebanon, John McCain spoke out against the measure even though he knew it would ultimately be approved.

issue, no matter what. Although he was definitely a Republican, he was not going to follow blindly any predictable path.

This was evident early in his term of office, when voting on a measure that would allow President Ronald Reagan to keep a peacekeeping force in Lebanon. The troops were there trying to stabilize the small Middle Eastern country that had been threatened by its neighbors, Syria, Israel, and Palestinian forces. In addition to its outside threats, Lebanon was divided by ethnic hostilities.

To try and stabilize the region, Reagan had sent 1,600 marines as a peacekeeping force. But the marines were restricted in what they were allowed to do. As peacekeepers, they were only allowed to fire if fired upon. This, McCain believed, was dangerous for the troops, as well as a complete waste of American resources.

Standing up for What He Believed

So in September 1983, when Reagan asked Congress for authorization to keep the force in Lebanon for another eighteen months, McCain decided to speak out against the measure. It was a largely symbolic gesture, and he knew it. The Reagan administration was powerful and popular, and the president had support of leaders in both parties. The measure would pass easily. But he believed he had to speak.

He told his fellow members of Congress that U.S. interests in Lebanon, whatever they may be, could not be achieved by a small peacekeeping force:

> The fundamental question is: What is the United States' interest in Lebanon? It is said that we are there to keep the peace. I ask, What peace? It is said we are there to aid the government. I ask, What government? It is said that we are there to stabilize the region. I ask, How can the U.S. presence stabilize the region?[64]

He reminded Congress that the situation was messy, and was liable to keep U.S. forces there indefinitely. "The longer we stay in Lebanon," he warned, "the harder it will be to leave. We will be trapped by the case we make for having our troops there in the first place."[65]

As predicted, however, Reagan's measure passed. But McCain had made a point. He had shown that he was his own man—that he could be counted on to speak out when he felt it was necessary. He would be loyal to the party on most issues, but he would not be silent on issues that he felt passionately about. The voters in Arizona were impressed, and voted him to a second term in Congress in 1984. And while he was gratified by their support, he had his eyes on a higher office.

Chapter 5

"A Breath of Fresh Air"

Almost immediately after the 1984 election, McCain and his staff started thinking about the Senate seat that was going to open up in two years. The seat was held by longtime Arizona politician Barry Goldwater. Because of advanced age, Goldwater was not going to run again. Being in the Senate would allow McCain to do even more important foreign relations work—which he loved—and might even lead someday to a presidential bid.

He announced his candidacy in March 1985, and prepared for what would be a difficult race against Arizona's well-liked governor Bruce Babbitt. However, Babbitt decided not to run in 1986, and McCain won easily against a less popular politician named Richard Kimball. In January 1987, McCain was sworn in as the new senator from Arizona.

"A Young Man in a Hurry"

Within his first months as a senator, he knew that the job was everything he had hoped it would be. "[F]or most of those first two years," he recalls, "everything seemed to exceed my expectations. I was generally regarded as an up-an-comer, someone to keep your eye on."[66] He was excited to be able to get on committees dealing with foreign policy as well as defense.

He worked hard to resolve one of the most troubling issues still lingering from the Vietnam War—the more than two thousand POWs and MIAs (Missing in Action) who were still unaccounted for, even fifteen years after the war ended. Because of his seemingly boundless energy and enthusiasm for the job, one August 1988 *New York Times* article called him "a young man in a hurry," as well as a "rising star."[67]

And although he was proud of his service in the Vietnam War, he insisted he did not want to let that be his only claim to fame. "I don't want to be known as the POW senator," he told one reporter in 1988. "What I've tried to do is position myself so that if opportunities come along, I'm qualified and ready. My job for the next few years is to acquire a reputation as a serious senator who studies the issues and doesn't try to steal the limelight."[68]

A Stirring Address

Even so, the limelight belonged to him on several occasions. As George H.W. Bush won the Republican nomination for president in 1988, McCain's name was on the short list for vice president. And while ultimately he was not the choice, he was chosen to give a key address at the Republican National Convention.

In that speech he described the heroism of a fellow POW who sewed a crude American flag from scraps of red and white cloth, using a bamboo needle. After the flag was discovered by guards, the man was severely beaten, McCain told the delegates. But when he was returned to his cell, the POW began sewing another.

The speech, which McCain used to demonstrate true heroism and devotion to country, made him an overnight sensation to the rest of the country who was not yet familiar with the new senator from Arizona. To political observers throughout the United States, McCain was definitely someone to watch.

John McCain was chosen to give a key address at the 1988 Republican National Convention in New Orleans.

The Absolute Worst Thing

But those initial successes could not make up for a scandal that arose in October 1989—an event, he told his staff, that was the absolute worst thing that ever happened to him. His aides were puzzled—how could it rank as the worst, they wondered, when McCain had endured torture and imprisonment for more than five years in Vietnam? "It can't be the worst thing," one aide protested. But McCain was adamant. "No," he insisted, "this is worse."[69]

The scandal became public in 1989, but in reality, it had begun two years earlier—just a few months after he was sworn in as senator. It had to do with Lincoln Savings and Loan, owned by a good friend of McCain's named Charles Keating. In the early 1980s, savings and loans, often called "thrifts," were given permission to invest depositors' money in real estate projects. However, Charles Keating and the owners of some thrifts were going too far. They were using millions of dollars of investments from customers to make extremely risky investments—so risky, in fact, that in many cases, they lost all their depositors' savings.

Hundreds of savings and loans went bankrupt in the 1980s because of such problems, and the federal government got involved. Federal investigators kept a close eye on those that were being run poorly or whose owners were making foolish investments.

In March 1987, federal banking officials were considering taking over Lincoln Savings and Loan to protect its investors from losing their money. Charles Keating did not want that to happen, so he turned to friends—politicians he had made generous donations to over the years.

The Keating Five

McCain was one of the five senators Keating contacted. He and the others did meet with federal officials about Lincoln Savings and Loan, as Keating requested. And those two meetings became important later, after the thrift finally went belly-up—costing

Three members of "the Keating Five"—senators John Glenn (left), Dennis DeConccini, and John McCain (right)—arrive for the Senate Ethics Committee hearings in Washington D.C., on November 15, 1990.

American taxpayers more than $2.5 billion to bail out its investors who had lost everything.

And when that happened, there was a great deal of publicity about Keating and his ties to those senators. Called "the Keating Five," they were pictured in the newspaper every day, alongside accounts of Keating and his reckless investing. Also published were the amounts of money Keating had donated to their campaigns. Many experts believed that the Keating Five had used their influence to delay the takeover of Lincoln Savings and Loan, and the Senate Ethics Committee did a thorough investigation.

McCain was angry—at Keating as well as at himself for trusting him. He admitted that he and Keating had been friends. But he maintained that he had done nothing wrong. He had not pressured bank officials to go easy on Keating, he told investigators:

> He was a supporter. I vacationed at his home in the Bahamas. He was one of the wealthiest men in the state of Arizona. He involved himself politically heavily in Arizona. That was the extent of my knowledge of his financial involvement in the state. And I was grateful for his support and his involvement in my political career. I had a friend. That friend wanted me to do something that was wrong. I refused to do so. That ended the friendship.[70]

"It Will Be on My Tombstone"

After a probe that lasted more than a year, McCain and another senator, John Glenn of Ohio, were found to have been guilty of only bad judgment. They had not acted improperly. The other three, however, were criticized more severely. One was censured, or officially reprimanded, by the Senate and his career in politics was virtually ruined.

While McCain was glad that he had been cleared, the incident had visibly shaken him. His brother Joe said that in some ways, the Keating scandal had affected him more than his time as a POW. "There had been something shaken in him," Joe McCain said. "He was used to trusting people. [In Vietnam] close friends had to trust each other. And here was a guy [Keating] who had gotten in under that radar."[71]

McCain himself admitted that the experience hurt him. Until the scandal, he prided himself on his good name. Even though he was not found guilty of wrongdoing, he felt this lapse of judgment would smear his name forever. "It will be on my tombstone, something that will always be with me, something that will always be in my biography," he said. "And deservedly so."[72]

Coming Back

McCain even thought about not running for his Senate seat again in 1992, but eventually decided to run. He threw himself into campaigning, an activity he really enjoyed. He imagined that the Keating scandal would be used heavily against him in the election, but it was not. He won easily, and he continued representing the people of Arizona in Washington.

McCain and Democrat Russ Feingold of Wisconsin (right) worked together to pass the McCain-Feingold campaign finance reform bill.

One project he took on in his next term was campaign finance reform. His experiences over the past year had demonstrated the problems caused by wealthy voters donating millions of dollars to candidates. Though many donors were simply trying to support their favorite party, in many cases they were using such donations to buy influence. They hoped that their contribution would pay off later—just as Keating had done.

McCain believed that the answer was to limit the amount of money that could be donated. He worked with Democrat Russ Feingold of Wisconsin to craft such a bill. It was very controversial among senators and members of Congress. After all, running a campaign was very expensive, especially with the high cost of television advertising. Many politicians depended on generous donations to pay for their campaigns. The McCain-Feingold bill, as it was called, did not pass right away. Eventually, however, it was made into law, something of which McCain was very proud.

The Maverick

His work on campaign finance reform got attention not only from the voters in Arizona, but across the United States. John McCain was becoming known as a force to be reckoned with—someone who was doing far more than collecting a government paycheck. He was interested in making things better—and as his work with Feingold demonstrated, he was reaching across party lines to do it.

Although he considered himself a good Republican, he was proud of the fact that he was not constricted by every view that was typical of his party. He was a maverick, and his record showed it. He advocated gun control, for example, and spoke out in defense of gay Americans. He spoke out against tobacco companies and advocated fining them for targeting young people. He worked hard to create a patients' bill of rights that would give every patient access to information about his or her condition, as well as choices about treatment options.

And though he was a thorn in the side of many in the Senate who disagreed with him, most found him one of the most

First in Line at Disney World?

When McCain was considering running for president in 2000, he wanted to make sure his family was comfortable with the idea. It would mean that he would be gone for long stretches of time when he campaigned. It would also mean that the family would be photographed more often. When it came to a family vote, everyone said yes except his youngest son Jimmy.

McCain recalls telling his son that it would mean more to him if the vote were unanimous. Jimmy thought about it and asked his father if the son of the president would get head of the line privileges at Disney World. McCain said yes, and Jimmy promptly changed his vote. McCain says that if he had been elected, he would have made sure Jimmy got that privilege. "It would have been an abuse of office, I know," McCain says. "But what could I do? I promised him."

John McCain, *Worth the Fighting For: A Memoir*, New York: Random House, 2002, p. 374.

principled men in Washington. "John McCain is a person of great strength and character," said John Edwards, a Democrat who worked with McCain on the patients' bill of rights. "He stands up for what he believes in, whether it's popular or unpopular. He's a breath of fresh air to work with."[73]

McCain for President

When President Bill Clinton's second term was coming to a close, McCain decided to run for the Republican nomination for the 2000 presidential race. His name was becoming very familiar to the American voters. He had recently been named one of

John McCain campaigned for the Republican nomination for the 2000 presidential election, but he lost the nomination to George W. Bush.

The Straight-Talk Express

McCain felt that a good way to get his message across in the 2000 presidential primary was to be available to the press as much as possible. McCain's campaign leased a large bus and christened it the *Straight Talk Express*. Reporters were invited—and even encouraged—to come on board and talk with McCain about any subject they wished, whenever they felt like it. "I sat in a red leather swivel chair in the back," he recalls, "with half a dozen or more reporters, rotated in shifts, surrounding me. I spent more time with reporters than with many of my aides. I took all questions, ducked nothing, and talked for hours on end." In 2007 McCain reinstated the *Straight Talk Express* in his bid for the 2008 presidential nomination.

John McCain, *Worth the Fighting For: A Memoir*, New York: Random House, 2002, p. 379.

the "25 Most Influential People in America" by *Time* magazine, and his family memoir *Faith of Our Fathers* was a best seller. It seemed that if he were ever interested in running for president, this would be the time.

His main opponent for the nomination was George W. Bush, the governor of Texas and son of President George H. W. Bush. McCain was hoping that his experience in the Senate would make him the more attractive choice in the primaries. He appealed to many moderate Republicans for his stance on social issues, and he started strong in the early New Hampshire primary, appealing to that state's voters who appreciated independent candidates.

The McCain campaign traveled on a bus that they named the Straight Talk Express. The name was to remind voters that McCain prided himself on answering questions honestly. He also gave reporters a lot of access for interviews by inviting them to ride along.

McCain and his wife Cindy in front of the "Straight Talk Express" campaign bus in 2007.

In the end, however, his presidential bid failed. While McCain did well in some primaries, Bush and his staff courted evangelical leaders like Jerry Falwell and Pat Robertson. They not only supported him, but they helped mobilize millions of conservative Christian voters. As it turned out, this block of voters was the deciding force. They deemed McCain far too moderate, and voted overwhelmingly for Bush.

Looking Back

The campaign had been decidedly negative. Groups supporting Bush had made attacks on McCain in a number of ads and phone polls. One attack that infuriated McCain was a telephone poll that shamelessly exploited racist attitudes and suggested that McCain was unfaithful in his marriage. The poll asked conservative voters whether they would vote for McCain if they knew he had fathered a black child. The truth was that McCain and his wife had adopted a baby from Bangladesh, whom they named Bridget, in 1991. Another ad warned voters that McCain had a Jewish friend who disliked Christians.

The ugly attacks—especially those on his family—infuriated him. The result was that he spent more time trying to refute them than doing what he had wanted to do, which was to tell the voters how he felt on important issues of the day. After the election, he wrote that he would most likely never run again for president:

> I did not get to be President of the United States. And I doubt I shall have reason or opportunity to try again. But I've had a good, long run—forty-four years. I could leave [politics] now, satisfied that I have accomplished enough things that I believe are useful to the country to compensate for the disappointment of my mistakes.[74]

One More Time

But as tempting as retirement might have been, McCain did not leave politics. He went back to Washington as a senator. On February 28, 2007, less than eleven months before the end of President George W. Bush's second term, McCain appeared as a guest on *The Late Show with David Letterman*. He told Letterman, "The last time we were on this program—I'm sure you remember everything very clearly that we say—but you asked me that if I would come back on this show if I was going to announce [my candidacy]. ... I am announcing that I will be a candidate for President of the United States."[75]

McCain believed that the single most important issue facing America was the war in Iraq. In 2007, the majority of the American people were against the war, and felt that President Bush had begun the war with false information—that Iraq possessed nuclear weapons. In the years since that was disproved, support for the war had eroded. McCain knew that most Americans wanted to end the war. "Americans are very frustrated, and they have a right to be," he told Letterman's audience. "We've wasted a lot of our most precious treasure, which is American lives."[76]

McCain's views on many issues, for example gun control and illegal immigration, do not always coincide with those of a traditional conservative Republican. Instead, McCain is thought of as a moderate Republican.

However, he said that he believed that U.S. troops should stay in Iraq. He had supported President Bush's plan to send twenty thousand more troops there—what was known as a "surge." Extra troops, combined with better equipment and supplies for the fighting men and women, he believed, could win the war. He reminded his audience that he knew firsthand what it was like to be fighting an unpopular war without the full support of the government. Many military leaders in Vietnam had been furious because of the limitations put on them by politicians in Washington. He believed the United States now needed to give the soldiers every chance of doing what they were sent to do. George Bush had not done that, he reminded them. But as president, McCain promised, he would.

"I'm Older than Dirt"

His stance on the war has not been the only challenge to the campaign. Many conservative Republicans (who support his stance on the war) have found several of his other positions intolerable. For example, McCain has been an advocate of gun control. And his position on illegal immigrants (allowing them a path to citizenship, rather than forcing them out of the United States) has infuriated many Republicans, too.

His campaign has had a number of other challenges, however. In the summer of 2007, it looked as though he was in trouble. The McCain campaign, which had never been awash with money, was almost broke. Several key staff members left and were then replaced. No one knew whether he would have the ability to continue. The Straight Talk Express, which had been reincarnated for the 2008 campaign, was retired, for it was far too expensive. McCain is one of the only candidates who travels in coach, rather than first-class, when flying.

Another issue that concerns some voters is McCain's age. If he is elected, he will be seventy-two years old when sworn in—the oldest president ever to take office. Some worry that his age will sap the energy needed to govern, and render him more likely to suffer health problems. McCain is not offended by such concerns. "I'm older than dirt," he jokes, "and have more scars than Frankenstein."[77] Other than stiffness from the injuries he suffered as a POW, he says, he has lots of energy and is in perfect health. He also says that his vigorous ninety-five-year-old mother, "shows how good my genes are."[78]

Is Mac Back?

McCain won the New Hampshire primary in January 2008, and was ecstatic. He loved seeing the signs "Mac is Back" in the cheering crowds. He vowed to his supporters that he was on the

On March 4, 2008, John and Cindy McCain celebrated the news that McCain had clinched the Republican presidential nomination.

road to the White House. By March 2008, McCain won enough votes in the primary elections to ensure his nomination as the Republican candidate in the 2008 election.

His enthusiasm, unwavering sense of duty, and humor were evident throughout the campaign. Whether talking with reporters (which he greatly enjoys) or debating serious issues with his political rivals, he says what is on his mind. And in a world where politicians spin their responses to appeal to whatever audience is in front of them, McCain is different. *New York Times* columnist David Brooks agrees. "I can tell you," he says, "there is nobody in politics remotely like him."[79]

Notes

Introduction: A Proud History

1. Telephone interview with the author, September 15, 2007.
2. John McCain with Mark Salter, *Faith of My Fathers*. New York: Random House, 1999, p. 79.
3. McCain, *Faith of My Fathers*, p. 18.
4. McCain, *Faith of My Fathers*, p. 20.
5. Quoted in "McCain to Lay Out His Case for 2008 Presidency", *Fox News.com*, April 24, 2007. www.foxnews.com/story/0,2933,268223,00.html.

Chapter 1: Young Johnny McCain

6. McCain, *Faith of My Fathers*, p. 107.
7. McCain, *Faith of My Fathers*, p. 70.
8. McCain, *Faith of My Fathers*, p. 100.
9. Quoted in Robert Timberg, *John McCain: An American Odyssey*, New York: Touchstone, 1999, p. 23.
10. McCain, *Faith of My Fathers*, p. 101.
11. McCain, *Faith of My Fathers*, p. 100.
12. Quoted in Paul Alexander, *Man of the People: The Life of John McCain*. Hoboken, NJ: John Wiley & Sons, 2003, p. 23.
13. Quoted in Alexander, *Man of the People*, p. 24.
14. McCain, *Faith of My Fathers*, p. 107.
15. Quoted in Timberg, *John McCain*, p. 24.
16. McCain, *Faith of My Fathers*, p. 112.
17. Quoted in Timberg, *John McCain*, p. 24.
18. Quoted in Timberg, *John McCain*, p. 25.
19. McCain, *Faith of My Fathers*, p. 112.
20. Quoted in Timberg, *John McCain*, p. 26.
21. Quoted in Alexander, *Man of the People*, p. 25.
22. Quoted in Timberg, *John McCain*, p. 31.

23. McCain, *Faith of My Fathers*, p. 116.

24. Quoted in Timberg, *John McCain*, p. 28.

Chapter 2: To the Navy

25. Quoted in Alexander, *Man of the People*, p. 29.

26. McCain, *Faith of My Fathers*, p. 111.

27. McCain, *Faith of My Fathers*, p. 118.

28. Quoted in Alexander, *Man of the People*, p. 30.

29. McCain, *Faith of My Fathers*, p. 122.

30. McCain, *Faith of My Fathers*, p. 123.

31. Quoted in Robert Timberg, *The Nightingale's Song*. New York: Simon & Schuster, 1995, p. 40.

32. Quoted in Timberg, *The Nightingale's Song*, p. 40.

33. Quoted in Alexander, *Man of the People*, pp. 29–30.

34. Quoted in Timberg, *John McCain*, p. 29.

35. Quoted in McCain, *Faith of My Fathers*, p. 151.

36. Quoted in Timberg, *The Nightingale's Song*, p. 42.

37. Quoted in Cathleen Decker and Mark Z. Barabak, "McCain's Course Hasn't Been Straight or Narrow," *Los Angeles Times*, March 3, 2000, p. 1.

38. McCain, *Faith of My Fathers*, p. 161.

39. McCain, *Faith of My Fathers*, p. 162.

Chapter 3: Service in Vietnam

40. McCain, *Faith of My Fathers*, p. 177.

41. McCain, *Faith of My Fathers*, p. 178.

42. McCain, Faith of My Fathers, p. 189.

43. John McCain, "How the POWs Fought Back," *U.S. News & World Report*, May 14, 1973, p. 47.

44. McCain, "How the POWs Fought Back," p. 47.

45. McCain, "How the POWs Fought Back," p. 47.

46. Quoted in Timberg, *The Nightingale's Song*, p. 119.

47. Quoted in Alexander, *Man of the People*, p. 54.

48. Quoted in Timberg, *The Nightingale's Song*, p. 121.

49. Quoted in Timberg, *John McCain*, p. 95.

50. Quoted in Alexander, *Man of the People*, p. 244.

51. Quoted in Timberg, *John McCain*, p. 96.
52. McCain, *Faith of My Fathers*, p. 344.

Chapter 4: Beginning a New Life

53. Quoted in Alexander, *Man of the People*, p. 78.
54. Quoted in Timberg, *John McCain*, p. 115.
55. Quoted in Alexander, *Man of the People*, p. 86.
56. John McCain, *Worth the Fighting For: A Memoir*. New York: Random House, 2002, pp. 13–14.
57. Quoted in Timberg, *John McCain*, p. 128.
58. McCain, *Worth the Fighting For*, p. 32.
59. Quoted in Timberg, *John McCain*, p. 137.
60. McCain, *Worth the Fighting For*, p. 34.
61. Quoted in Timberg, *John McCain*, p. 141.
62. McCain, *Worth the Fighting For*, pp. 62–63.
63. Quoted in Timberg, *John McCain*, p. 134.
64. Quoted in Timberg, *John McCain*, p. 148.
65. Quoted in Timberg, *John McCain*, p. 148.

Chapter 5: "A Breath of Fresh Air"

66. McCain, *Worth the Fighting For*, p. 122.
67. Susan F. Rasky, "Senator John S. McCain: Two Years in the Capital, But Already a Rising Star," *New York Times*, August 9, 1988, p. A16.
68. Quoted in Rasky, "Senator John S. McCain," p. A16.
69. Quoted in Timberg, *John McCain*, p. 173.
70. Quoted in Alexander, *Man of the People*, p. 137.
71. Quoted in Decker and Barabak, "McCain's Course," p. 1.
72. Quoted in Decker and Barabak, "McCain's Course," p. 1.
73. Quoted in Alexander, *Man of the People*, p. 339.
74. McCain, *Worth the Fighting For*, pp. 393–94.
75. Quoted in "McCain to Formally Announce Candidacy in April After Trip to Iraq," *USA Today online*, March 1, 2007. www.usatoday.com/news/washington/2007-02-28-mccain-bid_x.htm.
76. Quoted in "McCain to Formally Announce."

77. Quoted in Michael Kranish, "Addressing Age Issue: McCain Says He May Only Seek One Term," *Boston Globe*, January 3, 2008, p. A14.
78. Quoted in Kranish, "Addressing Age Issue," p. A14.
79. David Brooks, "The Character Factor," *New York Times*, November 13, 2007, p. A29.

Important Dates

August 29, 1936

John Sidney McCain III is born in Panama Canal Zone.

1954

McCain graduates from Episcopal High School.

1958

McCain graduates from the U.S. Naval Academy.

1965

McCain marries Carol Shepp.

July 29, 1967

During his first combat mission, McCain survives a tragic fire on the USS *Forrestal*.

October 26, 1967

McCain's plane is shot down over Hanoi, North Vietnam, and he is taken prisoner.

1973

The Vietnam War ends and McCain returns to the United States.

1977

McCain becomes a navy liaison to the U.S. Senate.

1980

McCain divorces Carol and marries school teacher Cindy Hensley.

1982

McCain is elected to the U.S. Congress, representing the First District of Arizona.

1986

McCain becomes a U.S. senator, representing Arizona.

1990

The Keating Five scandal ends.

2000

McCain loses the Republican nomination for president to George W. Bush.

2008

McCain wins the Republican nomination for president.

Books

Barbara Jane Feinberg, *John McCain*. Minneapolis: Millbrook Press, 2000. Biography of McCain aimed at middle school readers. McCain's time in Vietnam gets considerable coverage.

John McCain, *Worth the Fighting For: A Memoir*. New York: Random House, 2002. Excellent accounts of his own career, intermingled with portraits of some of his heroes—from baseball's Ted Williams to Arizona legend Barry Goldwater.

Kim O'Connell, *Primary Source Accounts of the Vietnam War*. Berkeley Heights, NJ: MyReportLinks.com Books, 2006. Age-appropriate, first-hand accounts of soldiers who served in Vietnam, of North Vietnamese, and of Americans who disagreed with the war.

Catherine Wells, *Political Profiles: John McCain*. Greensboro, NC: Morgan Reynolds, 2007. This 112-page biography is written for middle school readers.

Periodicals

Jill Abramson and Paul Duke, Jr., "The Keating Five: Senators Who Helped Lincoln S&L Now Face Threat to Their Careers," *Wall Street Journal*, December 13, 1989, p. A1.

Holly Bailey, "The Renegade Returns," *Newsweek*, August 6, 2007, p. 32.

John Heilemann, "Missing McCain," *New York*, July 23, 2007, p. 26.

John McCain, "Putting the 'National' in National Service," *Washington Monthly.com* October 2001. http://www.washingtonmonthly.com/features/2001/0110.mccain.html.

Web Sites

John McCain (www.johnmccain.com). This is the official website of the John McCain for President 2008 Campaign. In addition to current campaign news, it contains biographical information, pages of photographs of Cindy McCain and the rest of his family, and discussions concerning issues about which he feels passionate.

Time.com Campaign 2000 Newsfile (www.time.com/time/ daily/special/election). This is a special online edition about the 2000 presidential campaign by Time magazine. There are dozens of photographs of each candidate, as well as essays describing the Republican and Democratic conventions.

USS Forrestal Museum, Inc. (www.forrestal.org). This website contains a lot of information about the USS Forrestal, the aircraft carrier on which McCain served. The site has information, first-hand accounts, photos, and even sound recordings of the loudspeaker messages from the ship during the tragic 1967 fire.

VietnamWar.com (www.vietnamwar.com). This site contains a great deal of information on one of America's most controversial wars. It has information about the reaction to the war in the United States as well as firsthand accounts of POWs imprisoned in Vietnam during the war.

AP Images, 17, 23, 27, 29, 35, 37, 40, 43, 48, 53, 56, 61, 64, 66, 73, 75, 78, 80, 84

© Arnie Sachs/CNP/Corbis, 71

© Corbis Sygma, 59

Ed Clark/Time Life Pictures/Getty Images, 32

Getty Images, 45, 51

Scott J. Ferrell/Congressional Quarterly/Getty Images, 82

Terry Ashe/Time Life Pictures/Getty Images, 10, 13, 14, 20

Gail B. Stewart has written more than two hundred books for children and young adults. She is the mother of three sons and lives in Minneapolis.